I Am Fearfully And Wonderfully Made

Yvonne Carson

I Am Fearfully And Wonderfully Made
Copyright © 2012 by Yvonne Carson

ISBN 978-0-9795278-1-4

Printed in the United States of America

Table of Contents

4

Chapter 1

God Loves YOU!

God loves you no matter what you look like on the outside. His ultimate will for you is to be whole: spirit, soul, and body. The world is obsessed with physical beauty. Women, especially, are bombarded with images of what they perceive is beautiful and acceptable.

You see the messages of this everywhere: in magazines, on television, in movies, in books, and in the modeling industry. The message they send is clear; if you do not look like the women who are high fashion models or "sexy" movie stars, you are not considered beautiful but defective in some way and you are rejected instead of accepted for the person you are on the inside – the authentic YOU!

As a Christian woman, you must know who you are in Christ. Your identity is in Him. It does not matter what society says about your body or your beauty. Remember, God says, "You are fearfully and wonderfully made." And as the saying goes, "God don't make no junk."

When God created YOU, He said, "It is very good." God is more concerned about the condition of your heart. He never looks at your physical appearance to determine your worth or His willingness to use you.

First Samuel 16:7 (NCV) says, "But the Lord said to Samuel, "Don't look at how handsome Eliab is or how tall he is, because I have not chosen him. God does not see the way people see. People look at the outside of a person, but the Lord looks at the heart". God uses the foolish things of this world to confound the wise (1 Corinthians 1:27).

If you are physically out of shape, you are not stuck with what you do not like. You must decide to take action. Honor God with your body by deciding to eat more healthy wholesome foods, exercising, and drinking plenty of water.

Become proactive; inquire of the Lord how to best care for your body – His temple. He made you, and He is the best Person to get advice from on how best to honor Him in the way of diet and exercise.

The Holy Spirit is your Helper. Ask Him to be your personal guide, trainer, and teacher, and He will help you. You can do all things through Christ who strengths you. As you learn to love God more, you will learn to love and appreciate yourself more and see yourself as God sees you and not by the faulty world's perceptions of body image and self-esteem.

Remember, "Do not be conformed to this world, but be transformed by the renewing of your mind" (Romans 12:2). You must allow the Word of God to transform you into who He has created you to be in Christ from the inside out.

Chapter 2

I Am Fearfully And Wonderfully Made

The world says if I don't measure
34-26-34 and wear a size 2
My body is flawed in some way
Who are "they" to tell me
I don't measure up
That my body is not beautiful
When the God of the universe tells me
I am fearfully and wonderfully made!

You judge me because I don't fit
Your ideal of beautiful
Well, I've decided
I don't care what you think!
And why should I?
Who are you to tell me I'm not beautiful
When the God of the universe tells me
I am fearfully and wonderfully made!

Whether my eyes are big,
slant, or crossed
I'm still God's unique
one-of-a-kind design
I'm beautiful just the way I am!
Yes! I think I'm all that!

Why should I hide or feel ashamed
When the God of the universe tells me
I am fearfully and wonderfully made!

I may have kinky, straight, curly,
dreadlocks or gray hair
Who are you to define
the beauty of my mane?
When the God of the universe tells me
I am fearfully and wonderfully made!

Whether I'm Petite, Junior,
Misses, or Plus
My body size doesn't define my worth,
my beauty or self-esteem
I'm beautiful and I got it going on!

You say you disagree?
Well, I'm tired of what you think!
Why should I care?

When the God of the universe tells me
I am fearfully and wonderfully made!

My skin may be black, brown, yellow, red, or white
Who are you to tell me what color is
"better" or "superior"
Or what color is ugly or beautiful?

God made our skin as beautiful and colorful as the
rainbow!
You say your skin color is better?
I say there's none better just different?

You disagree?
Why should I care if you disagree?
When the God of the universe tells me
I am fearfully and wonderfully made!

Note Of Caution: The next time you judge a person by the way they look, remember these Scriptures. That person just may be an answer to your prayers or the link to your destiny!

"Do not look at his appearance or at his physical stature, because I have refused him"(1 Samuel 16:7).

"I will praise You, for I am fearfully and wonderfully made; marvelous are Your works, and that my soul knows very well" (Ps. 139:14).

Chapter 3

Woman Of Destiny Declaration

I Declare….

I am a Woman Of Destiny

I am healthy, wealthy, and wise

I am anointed and appointed by God

I am an ambassador for Jesus Christ

I am a Woman Of Destiny

I am walking in my purpose daily

I know who I am

I know where I am going

I am guided by the Holy Spirit every step of the way

I am a Woman Of Destiny

I am of the redeemed and I say so

I find favor and good understanding in the sight of God and man

I am upright; therefore, integrity is my guide

I am a Woman Of Destiny

I am rooted and grounded in God's love

I am strengthened with might through the inner man

I am blessed with every spiritual blessing in heavenly places

I am a Woman Of Destiny

I am accepted in the Beloved

I am righteous and blessings are on my head

I deal truthfully; therefore, I am God's delight

I am a Woman Of Destiny

"I have a Joshua-Caleb spirit

I see that all things are possible because I believe

I am moving forward and possess my Promised Land"

I am a Woman Of Destiny

"I live in the prosperity and Wisdom of Solomon,

The freedom and favor of David, and the faith of Abraham

Goodness and mercy follow me as the angels of God protect and encourage me"

I am a Woman Of Destiny

I decree and declare all these things over my life, in the of Jesus Christ, and so it! Amen!

Chapter 4

You Are Special!

You Are Special!

There is no one else like ycu

No one acts the same as you

No one smiles the same as you

No one shows love just as you do

No one can take your place

That is why you are special!

There is no one who looks like you

Tall or short

Big or small

Skinny or fat

There is no one else exactly like you

That is why you are special!

Everyone has feelings

Everyone has favorite things they like to do

Everyone has special talents they can use

But no one does it the same way as you

You are not special because of who
your father or mother is

You are not special

Because of where you were born

Or where you live

You are special because God made you in His image
and in His likeness.

You are special because Jesus gave His life to save
yours so you can live with Him forever!

You are special because God called you to do a very
special work that only you can do.

You are special because God made you to be a king
and priest.

You are special because God personally adopted you into His own family, making you His daughter.

You are special because you are an heir and joint-heir with your brother – Jesus!

You are special because you have been given authority "over the fish of the sea, the birds of the air, over every living thing that moves on the earth."

You are special because you rule and reign together with the Lord Jesus Christ, the Anointed One!

You are special because Christ is in you, the hope of glory.

You are special because you have been set free from the bondage of sin and death.

You are special because God chose you and appointed you to bear His fruit that your fruit would remain.

You are special because Almighty God dwells in you richly in all wisdom and spiritual understanding.

You are not special because of the way someone makes you feel or what you can and cannot do.

You are not special because someone buys or gives you "things" or because you have money and possessions.

The truth of the matter is you are special because God says so! Everything God says is so!

So, celebrate your special, unique self, for truly there is no one like you and that makes you very special!

Don't waste your time trying to be someone else. Embrace the person inside of you, for in God's eyes you are special!

Chapter 5

Bible-Based Affirmations

Using faith confessions or affirmations based on God's Word will help build your faith as a beautiful, anointed woman of God. Affirming and confessing these affirmations/confessions will absolutely cause your self-esteem to skyrocket as you come to believe them in your heart.

I encourage you to keep on speaking God's life-changing Words over your life every single day. And if you do not have the faith when you first start out, it will come if you stick with it no matter how you feel or what things look like in your life. "Faith comes by hearing and hearing by the word of God" (Romans 10:17).

1. I am free from frustration and worries because I cast all my cares on the Lord who cares for me (1 Peter 5:7).

2. I am free from the spirit of bondage because whom the Lord sets free is free indeed (John 8:32).

3. I am free from guilt and condemnation because there is no condemnation to those who are in Christ Jesus (Romans 8:1).

4. I am free from lack and insufficiency because my God supply all my need according to His riches in glory in Christ Jesus (Philippians. 4:19).

5. I am free from fear because my God has not given me a spirit of fear but of power and of love and of a sound mind (2 Timothy 1:7).

6. I am free from defeat because my God always lead me in triumphal procession in Christ Jesus (2 Corinthians 2:14).

7. I am free from what people say I can't do because I can do all things through Christ who strengthens me (Philippians 4:13).

8. I am free from the clutches of Satan because greater is He (God) who is in me than he (Satan) who is in the world (1 John 4:4).

9. I am free from sickness and disease because Jesus took our sufferings on Himself and carried our diseases (Matthew 8:17, NCV).

10. I am free from lack of direction for my life because God instructs me and teaches me the way I should go; He will guide me with His eye (Psalm 32:8).

11. I am free from my past life of sin and failure because I belong to Christ and He's made me a new creation, all things are new (2 Corinthians 5:17).

12. I am free from hopelessness about my life because God has a plan, hope, and a future for my life (Jeremiah 29:11).

13. I am free from feelings of abandonment because my God promises never to leave me nor forsake me (Hebrew 13:5).

14. I am free from anxiety because I have the peace of God that surpasses all understanding; He guards my heart and mind through Christ Jesus (Philippians 4:7).

15. I am free from worry because Jesus left me His peace and I let His peace rule in my heart (John 16:27; Colossians 3:15).

16. I am free from low self-esteem because I am fearfully and wonderfully made; I am made in the image and likeness of my God (Psalm 139:14; Genesis 1:26).

Chapter 6

I Am Declarations – 1

"You shall decree a thing and it shall be established to you"
(Job 22:28)

I Decree and Declare…

- I am now doing what God created me to do.
- I am worthy of love
- I am worthy of happiness
- I am a worthwhile person
- I love myself
- I am lovable
- I have strong self-worth
- I have high self-esteem
- I am special
- I am beautiful
- I am fearfully and wonderfully made

- I am unique
- I am gifted
- I am talented
- I am creative
- I am smart
- I am a fast learner
- I am an awesome communicator
- I am caring
- I take excellent are of myself
- I am expressive
- I am capable of doing what I'm called to do
- I am highly motivated and productive
- I am highly motivated and persistent when going after my dreams and goals

Chapter 7

I Am Declaration – 2

"You shall decree a thing and it shall be established to you"
(Job 22:28)

I Declare and Decree…

- I am wise
- I am gifted
- I am talented
- I am anointed
- I am valuable
- I am special
- I am a loving person
- I am kind
- I am respected
- I am intelligent
- I am powerful

- I am a giver
- I am a saver
- I am a wise investor
- I am appreciated
- I am responsible
- I am an excellent listener
- I am a fast learner
- I am sensitive toward others
- I am the apple of God's eye
- I am a favored child of God
- I am a child of God
- I am discerning
- I am proactive
- I am friendly
- I am a new creation
- I am honest
- I am holy
- I am trustworthy
- I am sanctified
- I am confident
- I am walking and living in my purpose daily
- I am wise when using my time
- I am prosperous

- I am productive
- I am authentic
- I am spiritually enlightened through the Holy Spirit
- I am an encourager
- I am encouraged
- I am a woman of positive influence
- I am highly creative
- I am a winner in every area of life
- I am one with God
- I am at peace with God
- I am healthy, wealthy, and wise
- I am strong in the Lord and in the power of His might
- I am a woman of integrity, uprightness, and honesty
- I am a wise businesswoman
- I am an inspiration to my family and friends
- I am an inspiration everywhere I go
- I am anointed and appointed by God
- I am reaching people around the world for Jesus Christ
- I am debt free

Chapter 8

I Am Declarations – 3

"You shall decree a thing and it shall be established to you"
(Job 22:28)

- I am bold as a lion
- I am a doer of the Word of God
- I am friendly and fun to be around
- I am content
- I am relax and at rest with God
- I am a lifetime learner
- I am super-glued to my God-given purpose
- I am an innovative and creative woman
- I am an anointed and successful entrepreneur
- I am blessed to be a blessing to others
- I am growing into a holy temple in the Lord
- I am being built together for a dwelling place of God in the Spirit
- I am rooted and grounded in God's love

Chapter 9

I Am Declarations – 4

"You shall decree a thing and it shall be established to you"
(Job 22:28)

I Decree and Declare...

- I am blessed with every spiritual blessing in the heavenly places in Christ
- I am righteous; therefore, my mouth is a well of life
- I am righteous; therefore, my memory is blessed
- I am righteous; therefore, blessings are on my head
- I am sealed with the Holy Spirit of promise
- I am made alive together with Christ
- I am God's workmanship, created in Christ Jesus for good works

- I am free from a poverty mindset
- I am free from the spirit of poverty
- I am free from the spirit of debt
- I am free from the spirit of lack and insufficiency
- I am worthy of love and affection
- I am in control of the choices I make in life
- I am loved and cared for by God
- I am willing to take calculated risks

Chapter 10

I Have Decrees and Declarations

I Decree and Declare...

- I have boldness and access with confidence through faith in Jesus
- I have been brought near to God by the blood of Jesus Christ
- I have the joy of the Lord, who is my strength
- I have peace
- I have God's wisdom
- I have love
- I have understanding
- I have the fear of the Lord in my heart
- I have power to defeat my enemies
- I have creativity and energy

- I have the mind of Christ
- I have divine health and healing
- I have strength
- I have covenant friendships and relationships
- I have more than enough of everything I need
- I have positive and inspiring relationships
- I have all the support I will ever need
- I have a prosperity mindset
- I have a lucrative business
- I have a success mindset
- I have a thriving and successful ministry
- I have good health and wealth
- I have an abundance mindset
- I have a hope and a future
- I have more than enough to give to help others
- I have goodwill, favor, wisdom, and understanding because God lives in me
- I have favor with God and man
- I have friends I can trust and count on for advise
- I have friends I can depend on for emotional support
- I have clarity of vision and purpose

- I have a great sense of purpose in my life
- I have what it takes to be a success
- I have a creative and innovation sprit
- I have the spirit of wisdom, knowledge, understanding and discernment

Chapter 11

Positive Self-Talk Affirmations

- I believe in the person God created me to be
- I attract great people into my life because of the anointing on my life
- I attract honest, loving, faithful people into my life because of the anointing
- I respect myself
- I give myself permission to have fun
- I give myself permission to play
- I give myself permission to make mistakes
- I keep moving forward no matter how many obstacles I encounter
- Focus, self-discipline, and motivation come to me easily and effortlessly

About The Author

Yvonne Carson is a native of New York City. She is a two-time graduate of Oral Roberts University, where she received a Master of Divinity degree in 2006, and a Master of Arts Degree in Christian Counseling in 2008. Her degree is Christian courseling has a focus on Marriage and Family Therapy. She completed her minister-in-training program from Greenwood Christian in Tulsa, Oklahoma where Bishop Gary McIntosh licensed her as a minister 2008.

Yvonne is an author, personal coach, trainer, and teacher. Her life is dedicated to helping hurting people around the world by combining her love for God and His Word, teaching, counseling, writing, and coaching.

Yvonne is the Author of two Amazon Top 100 Best-selling books (available in print, Kindle, and PDF ebook format).

1. "How to Discover Your Life Purpose and Stop Just Existing: A Woman's Guide to Living Life With Purpose, Passion, and Fulfillment. (Ranked #1 in the Spiritual Growth Category).

2. "I am Fearfully and Wonderfully Made" (Ranked #2 in the Self-Esteem Self-Help Category)

She is also the author of "Declaring God's Word: 101 Biblical Declarations Every Christian Mom Needs to Declare Over Her Children" which was also made Amazon's 100 Top Best-sellers list) and "Biblical Insights For Spiritual Transformation."

As a Christian mentor, adviser, and personal life coach to women, Yvonne helps women discover their life's purpose, learn to identify and uncover the obstacles that keep them stuck and help them move forward in life. She believes in empowering women to overcome these obstacles, through the help and empowerment of the Holy Spirit, who reveals past pains and unresolved issues.

Minister Yvonne has witnessed many women break through their hidden barriers and catapult into their God-ordained purpose and destiny.

As a woman passionate about her faith and the truths of the Bible, Minister Yvonne shares the power of healing past hurts through Christ's love with women everywhere. She lives the message she writes, teaches, and speaks about. She knows firsthand how the Word of God, when applied, can and does, transform people's lives and encourages them to be all God created them to be.

Minister Yvonne has a compelling story of past hurts, childhood neglect, sexual, physical, and emotional abuse. Her past struggles with low self-worth, low self-esteem, and negative self-image and mindset is the catalyst for her work with women who struggle with the same things that held her in bondage and captivity for decades!

Minister Yvonne is available for one-on-one and group coaching and counseling sessions. She strives to help women be transformed from the inside out -- spirit, soul, and body.

Minister Yvonne is a single mother of four adult children, and has eight grandchildren.

Personal Note From The Author:

Thank you for purchasing my book. I pray that it has been a blessing to you. I would love to hear from you about your experience reading this book and doing the exercises. I would love for you to share some of your goals you have established for yourself as a result of this book.

Please feel free to write your comments about this book and any prayer requests you may have. I will answer your letters personally and will pray for you. If you have a testimony as a result of reading this book and working through the exercises, please email me and let me know about it. I pray that God continue to bless and keep you in His loving care and under His divine protection.

In His service and love,

Yvonne Carson, M.Div. MA, MFT

http://yvonnecarson.com

yvonne@yvonnecarson.com

Minister Yvonne Carson is available for speaking at your event (s):

- Retreats
- Prayer Breakfasts
- Bible Study
- Workshops/Seminars/Conferences
- Group Coaching
- Private Coaching
- Biblical Counseling

Simply fill out the contact form on her website at http://yvonnecarson.com.

www.ingramcontent.com/pod-product-compliance
Lightning Source LLC
Chambersburg PA
CBHW060637030426

42337CB00018B/3393